YOU DA ONE

JENNI(F)FER TAMAYO

Sections of YOU DA ONE have previously appeared in tenderloin, Poetry, Mandorla: New Writing from the Americas, The Boog Portable Reader, Aesthetix, The Life and Death of American Cities, Everyday Genius, Best American Experimental Poetry (BAX), Birds of Lace, and Angels of the Americlypse: New Latin@ Writing. Special performances of YOU DA ONE have been staged at The Bratty Poetry Series, IRL, Cold Cuts Series, The Museum of Modern Art, Louisiana State University, What's So Hot Salon, The Bureau of General Services-Queer Division, and The New York Poetry Festival. Many thanks to the editors and curators for their early support of this work.

ISBN: 978-1-934819-67-8

Book design by Leah Sewell & Sarah Gzemski
Cover image by Sean Patrick Cain |seanpatrickcain.com
Proofreading by Monroe Hammond

PRAISE FOR *YOU DA ONE*

"I am addressable"—Jennifer Tamayo's YOU DA ONE, is a maliciously filial exploration of packaged familial relations. Professional Detail: suggest face-to-face interplay with the severed head of Gwenyth Paltrow in Se7en. Is that your daughter? Is she a box? Tamayo posits a slick surface of home and determinate location only to scrape it through a landfill of epistolary detritus, Spanglish, and pop music. Daddy-daughter playtime becomes a sweet serial narrative, caught and unraveling on the jagged edge of obedience. There is no manicured heaven here, nor any logic of quotation, simply the primordial spit of techno-banality from which emerges the thrill of the partial. Look into those $50 bona fide baby blues: you (the one) you're on a lawn, your hand is in a bowl of grapes. Look at the camera, darling, smile for Mommy in your best interior composition! –Trisha Low

By turns violent, political, romantic, incestual, cerebral, bodily, and personal, this second full-length from Tamayo (Red Missed Aches) bears the formal markings of the hypermodern in its deployment of digital, pop, and intertextual elements. Written after her first trip back to her native Colombia in 25 years, the book is indebted to Rihanna, Barthes, and Aimé Césaire, whose texts she mines voraciously. Those influences, as well as the spectres of Alfred Molina and the author's father, haunt the page, intermixed with screen captures, cheap internet advertising, deliberate misspellings, and pun-ridden Spanglish." –Publishers Weekly

Dear Reader,

One of the narratives of this reprinting of YOU DA ONE is that of refusal. Of NO.
Originally published in 2014, this new edition of YOU DA ONE is comprised from the
attempts to say NO to a gendered violence prevalent in my communities as it prevails
around the globe. The original publisher of this book played a role in people's suffering
and contributed to the ongoing silencing of survivors of sexual assault, none of which
I could support. There are details and names that are neither mine to share, nor crucial
to this moment of NO. My decision to withdraw the book from its original home was
not exclusively about one person, or one publisher or one instance. It was about
patterns and layers of trauma so deeply imbedded in our literary communities that it
will take many efforts, small and large, to begin to address and dismantle. Withdrawing
YOU DA ONE from its first publisher was, in my opinion, a small effort in what I know
will be a lifelong work. The end of rape culture will not be comfortable because, like
all struggles against violence and domination, it is deeply imbricated in the global
anti-blackness and the on-going settler colonial project that enmeshes so many lived
realities and in which I am implicated.

In many ways, YOU DA ONE is a book informed by terrors and traumas of what it's like
to be so figured, you are figureless: a *shimmerwound*, I like to call it. I see some of
these traumas in the omissions the book performs only for me. This, for example, is a
poem that did not make the final, original version of YOU DA ONE: the omissions the
book performs for only me.

A few weeks before the big trip, I conjure something terrible to
happen. My therapist says that I had no doing in this terrible thing.
That the terrible thing happens all too often to women. I believe
her when she's speaking to me. When she's being kind in an office
that has soft light and boxes of tissues at every turn. My only wish
is that there were more pillows in the room, & that she wouldn't

put her feet up when we talk of the terrible thing. But besides
that she is kind and I am happy to have her kindness after the
terrible thing. When I tell her about the big trip, she asks that I start
coming more often. Could I come twice, three times a week? Could
I come four times a week? Could I come everyday? Could I come
before work and during my lunch hour? Could I come for dinner
too? Could I come 3 times a day and for coffee after? Could I just
sleep in the office? I should just sleep in the office. Also, did I have
some kind of physical object that defined me? That I could hold in
my purse, my pocket throughout the day. -- -- -- -- -- -- ---- -- -- -- -- -- --
-- -   I wanted
to be awful. I wanted to be abject. To undo all the good things that
were my body and my life. I wanted to feel like a terrible thing. &
maybe I wasn't searching for exactly what I got but I was searching.

I know what made me (attempt to) edit this out: shame & denial. I remember feeling
that this passage would be too much for the book to handle. The book would become
something else that I wouldn't be able to fully explain: the embodied experience of
living through a violence that can't be figured/out. This passage appeared, I would
tell myself and my editors, to be "out of nowhere," or "not related to" what I had begun
writing. Now, rereading the text under a new light, a new dissettling/setting, I see
this violence everywhere in the book. The trauma can't be erased because it is in the
bones of the book. It's laced into the heart. I hear a screaming in some of these poems,
a working to reconcile that I was too many traumas braided, traumas surfacing and
seeing themselves in the shimmer of histories whose last refusal is irreconciliation. I/t
was too many NOs.

In the past few years, though, I have become even more things somehow. And this reprint, I hope, will be something else too. I hope this version of YOU DA ONE, complete with 'interruptions' of collaborative writings, Facebook posts, and community hand-outs I contributed to alongside colleagues between 2014 and 2016, will more fully express what this book has come to mean in my life; a scar. Our reading of YOU DA ONE must be like the story of its reprinting: interrupted, marred, uncomfortable and unfinished. I want us to not forget that for many moments in these particular years, in the same pitch as our mothers and elders, a momentary "we" screamed NO.

I.   I AM THE PART OF THE SKELETAL BONE OF YOU HOW

II.   DOES YOUR HEAD YOUR HATE YOUR BODY

III.   WHICH OF OUR ORGANS ARE THE MOST SIMILAR

IV.   IF YOU, THE FATHER, IS THE DEATH OF ALL THINGS,
       YOU LACK AT ME & FEEL NARCISSUS

V.   IN THE AGE OF THE NEW INTERNET WHO SHOULD I LOVE

VI.   WHAT IS IT TO HAVE FALLEN IN TO MULTIPLE PIECES AND HAVE THOSE PIECES
       SKITTLED

VII.   SIC SIC SIC SIC SIC

VIII.   ONCE I DANCED WITH A MAN YOU LOOKED LIKE AND I HAD RIPPED THE FACE
       FROM OFF YOUR BODY

IX.   IN THE TREMBLING MOMENT OF OUR FIRST EMBRACE I'LL KISS YOU SO I CAN
       UNDERSTAND
                A. BUT I'LL REALLY BE TRYING TO EAT YOU

X.   I LOOKED UP THE POEM "DADDY" BY SYLVIA PLATH BUT IT HAD ANYTHING TO
       DO WITH US

XI.   HOW DO YOU BEHAVE IN ME—EVERYTHING LIKE THE INTERNET

XII.   WHEN I TOUCH YOU TRANSPARENT, WE WILL FEEL ALL OUR BAGS OF ASHES

XIII.   I CAN SMELL YOU

XIV.   I REMEMBER THE SPINE OF THE BLANKET YOU GAVE ME AND THE MEMORIES
       OF MONEY

XV.   YOU ARE NOW A FAT MAN—HAVE YOU EATEN ALL THE CHILDREN

XVI.   IF WE TOUCH, LET ME BE THE TALLEST CREATURE

XVII.   THIS IS NO SINCERITY

XVIII.   I MAY SAY I HAVE NO INTEREST IN WHAT YOU DO & I WEAR A SHAMED WITH
       THESE PANTS

XIX.   DO INTRODUCE THE OEDIPAL HERE

XX.   THERE IS A CHEMISTRY I WANT TO KNOW ABOUT LIKE HOW YOU ARE MIXED IN MINE

XXI.   WILL YOU WANT TO KISS ME LIKE YOU KISSED MOM WHEN SHE WAS MY AGE

XXII.   HOW MANY CHILDREN & HOW MANY LEGS

XXIII. TO EASE THIS I WRITE A SCIENCE FICTION ROMANCE OF THE FATHER-DAUGHTER DANCE

XXIV.   WHAT IS IT TO HAVE A PENIS THAT MADE ME & I WILL WANT TO LOOK AT IT OKAY

XXV.   THESE ARE PHOTOS IN WHICH YOU SCOWL

XXVI.   EVERY PART OF ME IS FAMISHED- ESPECIALLY MY GOLDEN MEGAPHONE

XXVII. WHY DO YOU DRINK UNTIL YOU CAN'T EVEN STUTTER

XXVIII. I CAN BE OBSESSED WITH THIS BODY BECAUSE YOU CAN RIGHTLY SAY I MADE YOU

XXIX.   WHAT PART OF ME WOULD YOU LIKE TO HAVE

        A. MY FORHEAD MY LIPS MY STOMACH MY ANKLE MY NOSE IS ACHING

XXX.   WHAT WAS IT TO HEAR MY VOICE ON THE PHONE & WHAT GHOST AM I TO YOU

XXXI.   IF WE PUT ARMS ON THIS IT MAY TOUCH

XXXII. WHEN WE PLEASE LET'S MATCH UP BIRTH MARKS—THE HISTORY IS UTTERING

XXXIII. I REMEMBER ONCE YOU WORKED HARD TO BUY ME THAT WHITE DRESS WHY DID YOU WORK HARD TO BUY ME THAT WHITE DRESS

XXXIV. OH BABY BABY, HOW WAS I SUPPOSED TO KNOW

XXXV.   HIT ME BABY ONE MORE TIME

XXXVI. MAKE NO SENSE TO ANYONE BUT OUR HUMAN BODIES

XXXVII. HAVE NO FANTASIES; I AM YOUR FLESH HOOK OF THE FUTURE

XXXVIII. HOW COME I MUST LOOK AT YOUR FACE; IT FEELS LIKE A PUNISHMENT; THERE IS NO FUTURE

XXXIX. WHO ARE YOU NOW & ARE YOU WAITING TO DIE AS I EXPECT

XL. WHERE ARE THE SOUNDS FOR WHEN YOU ENTER AND I ENTER AND

XLI. I PICTURED YOU AS ALFRED MOLINA—WHY ARE YOU NOT ALFRED MOLINA

XLII. WHEN I WAS LITTLE I KEPT YOUR PICTURE UNDER MY PILLOW BECAUSE I REALLY WANTED TO AND I THOUGHT THAT WAS WHAT I WAS SUPPOSED TO DO AND THEN WHEN I LOST IT I ONLY FELT SLIGHT OFF

XLIII. YOU WON'T EXPLAIN ANYTHING ABOUT MY BODY &

    A. I WILL BE DISSIPATED BUT THE INTERNET IS STILL AROUND

XLIV. & THE DREADED QUESTION: ARE YOU HAPPY NOW AND IF NOT WHEN IS THE LAST TIME YOU WERE

XLV. ON THE PHONE, YOU ARE NOT MUCH OF A TALKER WHY IS THIS & ALSO I MAY BE AN ANIMAL

XLVI. WHAT MOVIES DO YOU LIKE WATCHING & WHAT DO YOU MAKE OF YOUR OTHER SONS

XLVII. I DON'T BELIEVE YOU ARE A VIOLENT MAN—WHY NOT

XLVIII. LIFE DOESN'T MAKE SENSE BECAUSE THE INTERNET DOESN'T MAKE SENSE-AGREE OR DISAGREE

XLIX. I HAVE TRIED TO KNOW YOU BETTER IN MY IMAGINATION—I WON'T APOLOGIZE

L. AIMÉ CÉSAIRE IS A PERSON I'D LIKE YOU TO READ BEFORE I ARRIVE & THEN I ARRIVE

LI. WILL THERE BE WINDOWS IN YOUR HOUSE AND IF SO CAN I CRAWL OUT OF ONE

LII. MAKE IT NAUSEOUS, I'M TRAVELING IN TIME

XCIII.   WHEN THE GIRL MEETS THE FATHER AND SHE SEES HIM FATTER

XCIV.   THIS IS THE BELLY I CAN DIG MYSELF OUT

XCV.   I HAVE YOUR LUGGAGE IN MY MOUTH LIKE SEMEN

XCVI.   THERE'S NOTHING WRONG WITH SEMEN

XCVII.   WHAT CAGE ARE YOU LIVING THAT YOU ARE SO SATISFIED

XCVIII.   WHICH LANGUAGE MOVED YOU SO FAR AWAY FROM ME

XCIX.   UH

C.   I'M YOURS WITH SEVEN FISTS BECAUSE THAT'S WHAT WAS LAID UPON ME ONCE

CI.   UH

CII.   I'VE GOTTEN SO FAT ON THE INTERNET I CANNOT PUT MY DRESS ON

PROLOGUE

"Is it kind or sick to make things that have a body & related question on the internet; what websites do you visit." ROLAND BARTHES

YOU
DA

ONE

JENNIFER TAMAYO, my love how are you. This is my first email in life and I do it for you. I'm worried about the winter as you are, write me. My phone is 57.324.963.55-34

te quiero mucho tu abuela,

Leonor

USPS - FAST DELIVERY SHIPPING 1-4 DAY USA; BEST QUALITY DRUGS
FAST SHIPPING USA; PROFESSIONAL PACKAGING
100% GUARANTEE ON DELIVERY; BEST PRICES IN THE MARKET
DISCOUNTS FOR RETURNING CUSTOMERS; FDA APPROVED PRODUCTS;
35000+ SATISFIED –CUSTOMERS
35000+ SATISFIED –CUSTOMERS
35000+ SATISFIED –CUSTOMERS
35000+ SATISFIED –CUSTOMERS
35000+ SATISFIED –CUSTOMERS
35000+ SATISFIED –CUSTOMERS

35000+ SATISFIED -CUSTOMERS

Dear Grandmother of Lions,

It's me JENNIFER TAMAYO! That's god to hear from you. It makes me happy to knot that you are thinking of me. Believe it or not always, I tinker of you (and the family) a lot. My mom told me a lot of you. During Christmas, I said I was in contact with you (and Marcel and Sun) and she was very happy a lot. We try to give, get his number, but I'm not sure if you nose it well. She still catches you Grandma with Cheetos (Cheating? Cheetahs?). The grandma of the ch---

I feel good. Like I said to Marcel, I live in Baton Rouge (for now) studied literature and poetry at the Universula of Louisiana. In May, I will finish my Masters and my boyfriend (and our drogs) will be moving to another city. We have a very nice life here---with a lot of friends and lots to do. We are both artists and work together on a lot of projects. During the weekends we like to cook (we are vegetarians), camping, reading, and go for dancing.

Why do you care about the writing? How's it going in there, you liar, er, lion?

I love you, Grandma. I hope everything got swelled. How pleasure communicate with you a lot. Kisses and hugs foreva.

much love,

JT

Jennifer Tamayo

September 30, 2014 ·

ENOUGH IS ENOUGH. cis and trans women poets of NYC, we are holding a community/consciousness-raising meeting at Berl's on Oct. 26th-- time TBD-- to discuss the lack of safety in our poetry community and our actionable next steps. more details to come but please save the date and spread the word.

JENNIFER TAMAYO, my love, I got your message, what joy to hear from you.
Grandmother of Cheetos was Julia, my mom, your bisbuela, who died last October. For me, it was very sad but our family has always accompanied me.
Tell of your mom and of your brother. Tell me about your husband, where is, how old.
Congratulations on your mastery of poetry!
Then write you again---I love you. Also,

AUTO FINANCING AVAILABLE. BAD CREDIT CAR LOANS 100% ACCEPTED

AUTO FINANCING AVAILABLE. BAD CREDIT CAR LOANS 100% ACCEPTED

AUTO FINANCING AVAILABLE. BAD CREDIT CAR LOANS 100% ACCEPTED

AUTO FINANCING AVAILABLE. BAD CREDIT CAR LOANS 100% ACCEPTED

AUTO FINANCING AVAILABLE. BAD CREDIT CAR LOANS 100% ACCEPTED

AUTO FINANCING AVAILABLE. BAD CREDIT CAR LOANS 100% ACCEPTED

AUTO FINANCING AVAILABLE. BAD CREDIT CAR LOANS 100% ACCEPTED

AUTO FINANCING AVAILABLE. BAD CREDIT CAR LOANS 100% ACCEPTED

AUTO FINANCING AVAILABLE. BAD CREDIT CAR LOANS 100% ACCEPTED

AUTO FINANCING AVAILABLE. BAD CREDIT CAR LOANS 100% ACCEPTED

Hello. Jenny.

Hope you are well--- I tell you that I will do the questions of the bank in Medellin--- I will contact you---

Write me anytime because you respond with great pleasure---

I love you--

Your Father

P.S. JENNIFER TAMAYO, my doubter, a hug and a thousand blessings on this day, may God preserve you for many more years. And---

DID YOU HEAR THE BIG SECRET?!!!

THERE IS A CHEMISTRY I WANT TO KNOW ABOUT
LIKE HOW YOU ARE MIXED IN MINE

a quick looksee-goosee at the glossy Lonely Planet Colombia Guide Book gives me a
vertigo that starts in my face ovaries but the man at Book Culture catches me by my hair
when I tumble into the pages of the Zona Rosa beaches & hystorical ruin
& sticks the Césaire book in my celestial baby wound!

This is knot the translation I ached for, sir
OR, "was [it] written in the shape of their pelvis"

OPRAH HAS A SISTER AND HER NAME IS PATRICIA!

JENNIFER TAMAYO, my girl, how these wills and we do not talk? I'm glad that you are going to graduate soon. I tell you that I have a granddaughter; Julia is five years old. I will send a photo. She is the granddaughter of the Sun.

I crochet, you know? With two needles, I make folders, scarves and balances.
Your dad is so totally happy that you rote.

JENNIFER TAMAYO, I send you a kiss and a hug. Write, okay? Write! Write us! You write about so many but never us. And please,

FIND SINCERE JEWISH SINGELS IN YOUR AREA

MEET ATTRACTIVE JEWISH SINGELS IN YOUR AREA

START FLIRTING!

START FLIRTING!

START FLIRTING!

START FLIRTING!

START FLIRTING!

START FLIRTING START FLIRTING START FLIRTING

No to rape
No to denying rape
No to gaslighting
No to drugging people at readings
No to sexual violence
No to relentlessly sexualizing
No to relentlessly gendering
No to misgendering
No to gender
No to decorum
No to forums
No to allies
No to enemies
No to individuals aren't the institution
No to individuals are the institution
No to gossip shaming
No to not speaking up
No to not naming names
No to blaming those who speak and those who name....

From no manifesto for poetry readings and listservs and magazines and "open versatile spaces where cultural production flourishes" after Yvonne Rainer

Signed: a crowd of feminists based in Baltimore, MD, US Berkeley, CA, US Brighton, United Kingdom Hamilton, ON, Canada London, United Kingdom Melbourne, Australia New York, NY, US Oxford, OH, US Oakland, CA, U.S. San Francisco, CA, US Vancouver, BC, Canada lacking consensus and okay with that

START FLIRTING .... NOW!

Daughter, JENNIFER TAMAYO,

I wish you a happy birthday!

I hope that it passes through your entire body very well and you enjoy a lot in your day.

I love you---a hug from your family here in Colombia---your grandparents---your uncles---your primos---your aunts---and your brother.

With sincerity,

Your Farthing.

Thanks, Dad.

God to hear from you on my birthday! I had a great---with---friends here in New York.

Hugs and kisses to everyone in Colombia.

JENNIFER TAMAYO

> P.S. All is good here, by the way. No need to worry. Our neighborhood lost no electricity or anything during the hurricane. (We live in the good part of the city).

¡OH JENNIFER TAMAYO! ¡Blessings of God! ¡Blessings of God! ¡Blessings of God! As we have seen and read very dramatic situations on the internet. I will comment et al. God fills you with his many blessings. God shoves all of his many blessings inside of you. A huge hug and kiss. When you get a chance, check out-- hi there, dear info! NY Sales

SUPERB QUALITY->>>>>>>>>>>>>>>>>>>>>>>>
Ciails - 1.71$
Viagar - 0.79$
Propecia - 0.29$
Leivtra - 1.68$
⊠ Free Delivery Insurance,
10 years WorldWide Supplier

24/7/365 Support, ~ 24/7/365 Support, ~
24/7/365 Support, ~ 24/7/365 Support, ~
24/7/365 Support, ~ 24/7/365 Support, ~
24/7/365 Support, ~ 24/7/365 Support, ~
24/7/365 Support, ~ 24/7/365 Support, ~
24/7/365 Support, ~ 24/7/365 Support, ~
24/7/365 Support, ~ 24/7/365 Support, ~
24/7/365 Support, ~ 24/7/365 Support, ~
24/7/365 Support, ~ 24/7/365 Support, ~
24/7/365 Support, ~ 24/7/365 Support, ~
24/7/365 Support, ~ 24/7/365 Support, ~
24/7/365 Support, ~ 24/7/365 Support, ~

24/7/365 Support, ~ 24/7/365 Support, ~
24/7/365 Support, ~ 24/7/365 Support, ~
24/7/365 Support, ~ 24/7/365 Support, ~

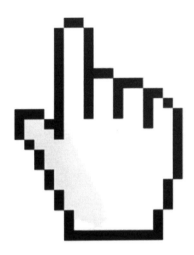

"I DON'T WANT TO TALK ABOUT IT, FOR FEAR OF MAKING LITERATURE OUT OF IT—OR WITHOUT BEING SURE OF NOT DOING SO—ALTHOUGH AS A MATTER OF FACT LITERATURE ORIGINATES WITHIN THESE TRUTHS."
RIHANNA

IF YOU, THE FATHER, IS THE DEATH OF ALL THINGS, YOU LACK AT ME & FEEL NARCISSUS

There's no lake or ocean around so I find my compact mirror & squatsquat.

Can this open section swallow. It's dirt hungry. Slurk hungy. Mod-daughter hungry. Bieber nipple hungry. So hungry I swallow my oh my! So hungry I swallow my oh nah-nah what's my name? So hungry I swallow my whole face. So hungry I'll swallow your hole face.

Where is the Palacio of the Inquisition? Who likes to drink? Colombians like to drink! Will you give me Hepatitis A? Who used to write me using a strange name? Do you hear the white world/horribly weary with its immense efforts?

I TURN BABY SO I CAN BE APPROPRIATELY READ:

always in veer, always rounding the corner

she coming into a contiguous state

BUT I HAVE THIS BODY SO

hey, little cut,

there is no refuge when you ENGLUUUUSH

when you prepare to meet your father, you are doubled over and two more times daughter. A construct in your doubled cut/over. http://en.wikipedia.org/wiki/Alfred_Molina

[Before the big trip, Jennifer rehearses in full costume: her face a blast in the shimmerwound. She will practice squealing. She will say hello fodder, put her head into the heap of his daddychest and smell the fodder over and over. You will lick yourself. Your cells will split open. Your skin will disappear.]

Lick yourself, don't you like yourself.

that we must learn for ourselves how to say NO and teach our beloveds how to say NO, like a NO beyond/under the breath, or a NO just at our homes with friends or on our blogs days later, and that the instinct to shout and spew NO NO NO in the moment and without hesitation (because our critiques have become so lucid and so fierce) becomes a reality, the expectation. in the same way we expect ourselves to listen to each other, we expect ourselves to spout NOs unapologetically when the moment arrives as it always does

and that the moment and the timing of our no's will be different because our survivals will be different

Jennifer Tamayo

June 2, 2015 · Instagram ·

THIS IS HOW MANY FUCKS I GIVE WHEN MY EDITOR TRIES TO INTIMIDATE, THREATEN AND SILENCE ME WITH HiS LETTERS FROM HIS LAWYERS. I won't be taking shit down from my wall or maybe I will. Don't forget me when I'm deported. ▫

[Her skin will disappear. Her cells will split open.]

There's no WE here   there's barely an I

& all my eye roll into myself
I will stay here in this desire network & my spitting image
when I see you, DA, I did a little bit death
your face a lock

You drape your genitals over me
when you watch me so
Your face à la

INTERNET LINKS

You left your mark on a whole generation. You would arrive in a pink spaceship and every kid would want to fly off with you. Children all over Brazil would rush to have breakfast to the sound of your song, Who Wants a Bread Roll? Another symbol of the times was the "Xuxa kiss," where you would leave your mark in lipstick. Your were a happy break. Apart from enjoying yourself, you always put across positive messages to the public with phrases like: "Wanting is believing and getting!," "Chase after your dream!," "Drugs are bad!" and many more.

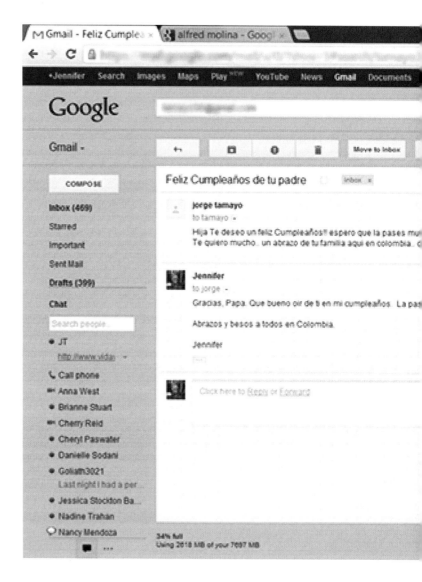

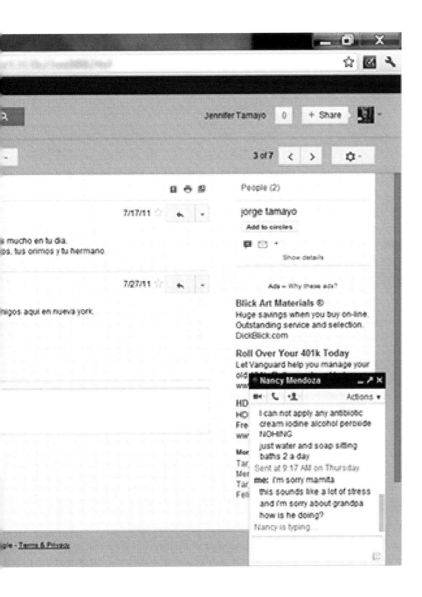

No to my white idols
No to your white idols
No to the bodies their fame drags in their wake
No to you when you do not denounce them
No to your obfuscation
Not to fairness, No to balance, also,
No to white people, in general
No to white feminism, in general
No the ways in which I couldn't see my own white feminism
No to thinking when i say white i mean fair skinned
No to white fragility
No to making me explain white fragility to you

In my face, you're a spitting—

Because there's the body

there's a safety handle in the airplane bathroom

& i shit like I've never shit before
i am more shit than body
every living thing, a pulp inside me
when you hear me squealing
remember it's the national hymo
oh nah nah what's my name, what's my name

SIC SIC SIC SIC SIC

ONCE I DANCED WITH A MAN YOU LOOKED LIKE AND I HAD RIPPED THE FACE FROM OFF YOUR BODY

Oh my!

Oh my!

Oh my,

darling imaginations

Ten days before the big trip, you consider an eating disorder. You need to make room. A space so large you could fit several people & animals. You don't care if they fit comfortably. Cram them in, she thought. Cram them in. Cut their limbs off. Put their bodies through a strainer. Liquefy the people & animal bodies. You dream of hot entrails! They don't need to be comfortable, you think, just fit inside. Stop eating all of your favorite foods. No more baked potatoes, popcorn, or Kit-Kats.

By the third day, you have only lost a pound and a half. I am so hungry I can speak a thousand! But god will make my holes large, you think. God loves my holes and I love god!

SICK BITCH
by the daughter

Imma SICK BITCH
and I will be for another few years
then I won't be any more
You can only play SICK BITCH until you are 19 or maybe 20
it can come out if you're physically ill
cancer, maybe
or being 5 months pregnant
otherwise get your SICK BITCHness into the closet (lol)
it can also come out on Thanksgiving
& holidays that involve eating

Here's a story about how SICK BITCHes get made:

I need a bigger size Jody mumbled to the lady at American Apparel.
She gave Jody a blank look. Jody repeated a little louder: I need a
bigger size, please! Don't worry, honey, said the lady, everyone needs
a bigger size at American Apparel. Jody shut the door and cried snot
into the baby spandex jumper with the little gold stars
& then she didn't buy it.

POOR HUMAN JODY
POOR HUMAN JODY
POOR HUMAN JODY
POOR HUMAN JODY [etc. read until out of breath].

The end.

SICK BITCH syndrome
it got me good on the plane ride on the big trip
while I was watching a Ben Affleck movie
passing over Panama

I'm not okay

I'm not okay

I'm not okay

I said finally
to the stewardess

There's no WE here   there's barely an I

[In the trembling moment of first embrace,

I rip the face off a Grace Kelly]

I change into a black polka dot

[In the trembling moment of first embrace, I rip the face off a Grace Kelly]

I hugged him I sunk in to the screen {

sink into the dot

I beckoned him cuz I saw my faces} I sunk into the screen {

His face looked dead/I was dead to see his face I sunk into the screen {

Grace Kelly Patron Saint of First Addressings {

Grace Kelly Patron Saint of Only Daughters & Secret Fathers

Grace Kelly Patron Saint of Unholy Human Shits

Bless me now

In the trembling moment of first embrace

In the trembling moment of first embrace I thought this is special this is special this is so fucking special. Jennifer, darling, don't forget this special fucking moment for the rest of your life.

In the trembling moment of first embrace nothing collapsed in me

Or in to his body, though I felt fatter.

**I THOUGHT YOU WOULD LOOK LIKE ALFRED MOLINA
WHY DON'T YOU LOOK LIKE ALFRED MOLINA**

I looked up the poem "Daddy" by Sylvia Plath but it had anything to do with us

The deer transformed into human head. The head had brains. The head had horns. The head had ears long like a liars. They shot the deer body. Dear body, had 5 arrows for each corner of the earth. She was running away away that deer body & could not get away from head. It had no desire in being a human head any more. But head can't do without body. That dear head.

HOW DO YOU BEHAVE IN ME—EVERYTHING LIKE THE INTERNET

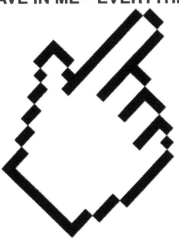

When I touch you transparent, we will feel all our bags of ashes

Oh my
Oh my
Oh my

Darling imagination, I don't want to put you to the grave but here come the real bodies.

Oh my
Oh my
Oh my

I think the speaker's father is dead. I think the speaker's mother is dead. I think the speaker is about to die. I think the speaker's father is not the father but the boyfriend. Yes, I think all the you's are the boyfriends. I think the speaker shouldn't write this until the father and the mother are both dead. I think the speaker is a figure of speech. I think the speaker is foreign. The language sounds foreign. I think the speaker is almost at the moment of a death but not quite yet. I don't think the speaker believes in sincerity. I think the speaker should take out the boyfriends.

THE DAUGHTER IS A TYP-O-MISERY

And we are standing now, DADDY and I, hair in the wind, my DADDY puny in its enormous fist and the DADDY is not in us but above us, in a voice that drills the DADDY and the DADDY like the penetrance of an apocalyptic wasp.

SO I MAKE SURE I BEHAVE

SO I MAKE SURE I BEHAVE

SO I MAKE SURE I BEHAVE

I AM NOW A FAT MAN—I HAVE EATEN ALL THE CHILDREN

& when I englash you!
how did my long intestine get on my shoes
I need a new dress
from American Apparel
something latex to keep
all my entrails in

No to non-apologies, apologies full of excuses, apologies blaming others, apologies all about yourself or your own guilt-driven need to explain at length
No to defensiveness
No to decorum
No to forums
No to panels
No to roundtables
No to any forum, panel, or roundtable that does not discuss these issues
No to being a man who just wants to "move on"
No to not dealing with the mess after

From no manifesto for poetry readings and listservs and magazines and "open versatile spaces where cultural production flourishes" after Yvonne Rainer

Signed: a crowd of feminists based in Baltimore, MD, US Berkeley, CA, US Brighton, United Kingdom Hamilton, ON, Canada London, United Kingdom Melbourne, Australia New York, NY, US Oxford, OH, US Oakland, CA, U.S. San Francisco, CA, US Vancouver, BC, Canada lacking consensus and okay with that

THIS IS NO SINCERITY

always in veer, always rounding the corner

of your other othered on the internet

there is no refuge in my ENGUUUUUSHH

cuz I'm a cut, a glossy shimmerwound

can you feel me/cut me

can you feel me revising the theory of multitudes

I don't contain them

I [STUTTER] AM THEM

did you see me on the internet

There's no WE here,   there's barely an I

WHERE IS THE SHIMMERWOUND

What is it to have a penis that made me & I will want to look at it okay

No to not feeling your own shame
No to understanding the power of shame
No to so much shame you can't speak
No to so much shame that maybe you don't speak
No to only publicly speaking your shame
to speak our shame publicly is an effort towards comfort
No to comfort

THESE ARE PHOTOS IN WHICH YOU SCOWL:
CHELSEA CLINTON
ANASTASIA TREMAINE
DRIZELLA TREMAINE
CINDERELLA —
NO LAST NAME
SOFIA COPPOLA
NADIA COMANECI
IPHIGENIA
DOLORES "LOLITA"
HAZE
MELANIE DANIELS
CATHY BRENNER
CATHY (CARTOON)
VIRTUALLY ALL
CATHY'S WITH A C
KOURTNEY AND KIM
KARDASHIAN
JANET JACKSON
ELEKTRA

71

KATE HUDSON
CLAUDETTE
JODIE SWEETIN
WISALAWA
SZYMBORZKA
MOBY DICK
LISA SIMPSON
BRIAR ROSE
MADELINE FOGG
DAUGHTER OF
DOROTHY FROM
WIZARD OF OZ
KERRI STRUG
BOBBI CHRISTINA
BROWN
DONNA JO TANNER
MICHELLE TANNER
(NOT STEPHANIE
TANNER)

LAILA ALI
PARIS JACKSON
PRINCES DI
KATNISS EVERDEEN
MARIE ANTOINETTE
SHIRLEY TEMPLE
RITA HAYWORTH
JAMIE LEE CURTIS
VERUCA SALT
SURI CRUISE
SARAH PLAIN & TALL
BRISTOL PALIN
MAYBE PRINCESS
BELLE
PUNKY BRUSTER
MARISA CRAWFORD
& THE MENENDEZ
BROTHERS

At the airport, we all take a shot of aguardiente

because we all had each other's faces

When I saw my brother I saw my face

I saw my grandmother I saw my face

I saw my aunt I saw my stupid face

On the way up the mountain I saw my face in a pile of trash

I saw my face in the mule's ass

I saw my lover I saw my face but it was white & weary

I saw my brother again and there was my face;

        my other brother, my other face

I saw my face in the American Apparel ivory chiffon blouse

I brought for this occasion

In the occasion I saw my face, I did

I saw my face in the pankekees the next morning

My face was in the talk of death

My face was in her teeth, the pavement, etc.,

There was a jail cell at The Museo Nacional, I saw my face

A woman flowercunted & crosslegged, my face & my face

Everywhere my face like I didn't have one

Botero's asses all my faces

I took down notes when it came to torture

& the inquisition and saw my face in the leather swing set

Clavicle spikerest & eye ruptrest

Faces, I suppose, are a type of torture

to look like one but never be one

* * *

When I got back to New York, I saw my face again

in the gutter of the C train

I saw a black face & I saw my face

It bleed, my faces

and I saw my face and your face was there too

I saw his face with freckles there was my face

there was tenderness so I ripped off the face

from off the earth and it was not a face

It was trash

I saw a green thing ENGUUUUSHING I saw my face

We had their faces and our faces and their faces were falling

I saw the white hole deep I saw my face

Did you see my face when you stepped on it

It was my face

I licked the screen and it was my face I liked my face

I ran the cursor over his face and it was our faces

I sat on your face I saw my face

I sat on her face and my face turned into my face

I saw the surface and it was my face

I saw my face and I saw the deepest lettering

There were words and my face was in the words

On your taint, your tethering I saw my face

You stuck that in me and my face was there

I saw my face when you turned over & over

My face was still there and there and it was your face too

I took off your face and you felt better

You said I fell better

I fell so much better

I CAN BE OBSESSED WITH THIS BODY BECAUSE YOU CAN RIGHTLY SAY I MADE YOU

I skum magazines, blogs, my favorite books for the parts in which I can see myself & clutch me like a shard. Fish for a thing that mirrors cuz the language shimmers at the spot in which it hooks. I do this too with emails from lovers, fathers, spam from the internet, your text messages. Things that I want to get pricked by. Even with words that I myself have written—I want to clutch me. Trap my body between sounds and meaning. Not knowing this tripping will turn to a skinning. The stuff is made of machetes and I let the body drop most gracefully upon it.

For example, once, after a lover said he just wanted to be friends, I ran into the Barnes & Nobles & opened up all the books by Murakami & put my mouth, my gums on them & bled out in total ecstasy in one of the back aisles. I got so culled.

you, run my hand past this page like it is a field; I want to be your bloody English thug. Lay this book on my tits, my belly, my ankles & let the words hook on my skin until I'm all fleshy. This feels wonderful & I feel alive. I lay this book on my face & it pulls at all my openings. Its carnations open me like the bell I am.

Consider, after consumption, my limb will grow in you

Nothing comes without its own wantings

Consider the root corrupted, the sentence fragment

Consider the prism of your sexual organ—deflecting a light

Consider the cursor: obliterative, total

& IN THE MORNING YOU WAKE UP TRYING TO RECOLLECT THE DIALOGUE
FROM THE TREMBLING MOMENT OF FIRST EMBRACE

if you dwell on the message you won't ever get anywhere

are you dead

where is your face

did you lose your face again, Jennifer

what is the message and why are you going there

the dialog is saying you are lonely

which someone told you never to say

in a poem

Jennifer Tamayo

December 11, 2014 ·

I HAVE NOT FORGOTTEN that 3 women poets were drugged at a Copula reading last spring. HAVE YOU?

I'm lonely I'm lonely I'm lonely I'm lonely I'm lonely I'm lonely I'm lonely I'm lonely I'm lonely
I'm lonely I'm lonely I'm lonely I'm lonely I'm lonely I'm lonely I'm lonely I'm lonely I'm lonely
I'm lonely I'm lonely I'm lonely I'm lonely I'm lonely I'm lonely I'm lonely I'm lonely I'm lonely
I'm lonely I'm lonely I'm lonely I'm lonely I'm lonely I'm lonely I'm lonely I'm lonely I'm lonely
I'm lonely I'm lonely I'm lonely I'm lonely I'm lonely I'm lonely I'm lonely I'm lonely I'm lonely
I'm lonely I'm lonely I'm lonely I'm lonely I'm lonely I'm lonely I'm lonely I'm lonely I'm lonely
I'm lonely I'm lonely I'm lonely I'm lonely I'm lonely I'm lonely I'm lonely I'm lonely I'm lonely
I'm lonely I'm lonely I'm lonely I'm lonely I'm lonely I'm lonely I'm lonely I'm lonely I'm lonely
I'm lonely I'm lonely I'm lonely I'm lonely I'm lonely I'm lonely I'm lonely I'm lonely I'm lonely
I'm lonely I'm lonely I'm lonely I'm lonely I'm lonely I'm lonely I'm lonely I'm lonely I'm lonely
I'm lonely I'm lonely I'm lonely I'm lonely I'm lonely I'm lonely I'm lonely I'm lonely I'm lonely
I'm lonely I'm lonely I'm lonely I'm lonely I'm lonely I'm lonely I'm lonely I'm lonely I'm lonely
I'm lonely I'm lonely I'm lonely I'm lonely I'm lonely I'm lonely I'm lonely I'm lonely I'm lonely
I'm lonely I'm lonely I'm lonely I'm lonely I'm lonely I'm lonely I'm lonely I'm lonely I'm lonely
I'm lonely I'm lonely I'm lonely I'm lonely I'm lonely I'm lonely I'm lonely I'm lonely I'm lonely
I'm lonely I'm lonely I'm lonely I'm lonely I'm lonely I'm lonely I'm lonely I'm lonely I'm lonely
I'm lonely I'm lonely I'm lonely I'm lonely I'm lonely I'm lonely I'm lonely I'm lonely I'm lonely
I'm lonely I'm lonely I'm lonely I'm lonely I'm lonely I'm lonely I'm lonely I'm lonely I'm lonely
I'm lonely I'm lonely I'm lonely I'm lonely I'm lonely I'm lonely I'm lonely I'm lonely I'm lonely
I'm lonely I'm lonely I'm lonely I'm lonely I'm lonely I'm lonely I'm lonely I'm lonely I'm lonely
I'm lonely I'm lonely I'm lonely I'm lonely I'm lonely I'm lonely I'm lonely I'm lonely I'm lonely
I'm lonely I'm lonely I'm lonely I'm lonely I'm lonely I'm lonely I'm lonely I'm lonely I'm lonely
I'm lonely I'm lonely I'm lonely I'm lonely I'm lonely I'm lonely I'm lonely I'm lonely I'm lonely
I'm lonely I'm lonely I'm lonely I'm lonely I'm lonely I'm lonely I'm lonely I'm lonely I'm lonely
I'm lonely I'm lonely I'm lonely I'm lonely I'm lonely I'm lonely I'm lonely I'm lonely I'm lonely
I'm lonely I'm lonely I'm lonely I'm lonely I'm lonely I'm lonely I'm lonely I'm lonely I'm lonely
I'm lonely I'm lonely I'm lonely I'm lonely I'm lonely I'm lonely I'm lonely I'm lonely I'm lonely
I'm lonely I'm lonely I'm lonely I'm lonely I'm lonely I'm lonely I'm lonely I'm lonely I'm lonely
I'm lonely I'm lonely I'm lonely I'm lonely I'm lonely I'm lonely I'm lonely I'm lonely I'm lonely

I'm lonely I'm lonely I'm lonely I'm lonely I'm lonely I'm lonely I'm lonely I'm lonely I'm lonely
I'm lonely I'm lonely I'm lonely I'm lonely I'm lonely I'm lonely I'm lonely I'm lonely I'm lonely
I'm lonely I'm lonely I'm lonely I'm lonely I'm lonely I'm lonely I'm lonely I'm lonely I'm lonely
I'm lonely I'm lonely I'm lonely I'm lonely I'm lonely I'm lonely I'm lonely I'm lonely I'm lonely
I'm lonely I'm lonely I'm lonely I'm lonely I'm lonely I'm lonely I'm lonely I'm lonely I'm lonely
I'm lonely I'm lonely I'm lonely I'm lonely I'm lonely I'm lonely I'm lonely I'm lonely I'm lonely
I'm lonely I'm lonely I'm lonely I'm lonely I'm lonely I'm lonely I'm lonely I'm lonely I'm lonely
I'm lonely I'm lonely I'm lonely I'm lonely I'm lonely I'm lonely I'm lonely I'm lonely I'm lonely
I'm lonely I'm lonely I'm lonely I'm lonely I'm lonely I'm lonely I'm lonely I'm lonely I'm lonely
I'm lonely I'm lonely I'm lonely I'm lonely I'm lonely I'm lonely I'm lonely I'm lonely I'm lonely
I'm lonely I'm lonely I'm lonely I'm lonely I'm lonely I'm lonely I'm lonely I'm lonely I'm lonely
I'm lonely I'm lonely I'm lonely I'm lonely I'm lonely I'm lonely I'm lonely I'm lonely I'm lonely
I'm lonely I'm lonely I'm lonely I'm lonely I'm lonely I'm lonely I'm lonely I'm lonely I'm lonely
I'm lonely I'm lonely I'm lonely I'm lonely I'm lonely I'm lonely I'm lonely I'm lonely I'm lonely
I'm lonely I'm lonely I'm lonely I'm lonely

Are you dead yet

Where is your face going

Did you lose the message and get there

Dwell on your face, okay

IF WE PUT ARMS ON THIS IT MAY TOUCH

No to poetry if it's excusing you from acting, cuz you know poetry is enuf right?

INSERT IMAGE OF RIHANNA IN COLOMBIAN DRAG FUSTING MY DAD ON THE INTERNET

WHEN WE PLEASE LET'S MATCH UP BIRTH MARKS—THE HISTORY IS UTTERING

When I ask my father about her, how she was when she was my age

he uses the word temperamental

& there's a funny slip in my bowels

your mother, she also had hair

your mother, she also had hands

your mother, she was temperamental

In the other's language—the pang of this word falls on my metals

& my bowels slip and my bowels slip

I'm addressable. Even through time and bodies that are not my own, I'm addressable.

He laughs while I leave a stain on the couch

RiRi love IS so complicated

I REMEMBER ONCE YOU WORKED HARD TO BUY ME THAT WHITE DRESS
WHY DID YOU WORK HARD TO   BUY ME THAT WHITE DRESS

INSERT IMAGE OF JENNIFER IN THE WHITE DRESS
INSERT NOTES ON PUNCTUM
INSERT NOTES ON THE SHIMMERWOUND

My loneliness is killin' me
I must confess I still believe
When I'm not with you I lose my mind
Give me a sign, hit me baby one more time

Read more: **BRITNEY SPEARS—BABY ONE MORE TIME LYRICS**

My grandmother puts her hand into the juicer and says there are even juices made from flesh.

HAVE NO FANTASIES; I AM YOUR FLESH HOOK OF THE FUTURE

When she spits blood into the toilet

That's the best poem you've ever written

HOW COME I MUST LOCK AT YOUR FACE; IT FEELS LIKE A PUNISHMENT

Jennifer Tamayo

March 20 ·

WHAT THE FUCK. The end of rape culture will not be comfortable. Dear _____,_____, and _____: Please stop asking for "details." Please stop invoking "ethics" so you can silence survivors. Please stop telling survivors how to navigate their experience of assault and abuse. Please stop trying to save your image, your book, your organization, your legacy because uhhhh rape culture is "a complicated issue." #fireVIDAsfounders

No to poetry if it's excusing you from acting, cuz you know poetry is enuf right?
No to not making poetry enemies, there are enemies here
No to avoiding what it feels like to have an enemy, i need direction
No to me, i am probably an enemy of poetry
No to poetry that has no interest in liberation
No to those of you threatened by the word liberation
No to those of you who haven't considered liberation because you don't have to
No to those parts of us too scared to consider liberation
No to your aesthetics if they deflate the conversation
No to my aesthetics-- they have deflated the conversation

THERE IS NO FUTURE

& by chance, I have the baby in the bathroom in the middle of the night; I tuck her into one of these dents in the concrete and leave to go back to bed. I feel a little awkward so I go back to adorn my baby with a pair of fresh pearl earrings I had bought in Turkey a few summers ago with my now ex-boyfriend who is currently a consular officer in Chile or maybe Angola. Not sure exactly but we had laughed over the phone when he told me because one time I had told him that it was consular officers, young, cute American boys like him that had turned my family away at the border. Prisoned, in fact, my mother and me. We laugh: HA HA HA HA HA HA—but like in a real way… and now he's the one with the Three Suit Rule scribbled on the inside of his consular cubicle—more of a real joke, I suppose. It is, after all, the custom with newborns but my baby won't go to sleep, won't stop, not crying, not wailing, but grumbling, gurgling, gorging and I'm worried she'll wake up my grandmother and father and brother and father and uncle and uncle and aunt, lovely folks I've just met hours ago, and the house lady, Maria, who's been, perhaps, we think, stealing, she'll be awoken too by my newborn's gorges. In my uncle uncle uncle's house their house lady, Dolores, sleeps in room that's the size of a closet but they live in a gated community in the outskirts of Bogotá so it's quite a nice closet with a window that looks out to the rose bush. But still, when we leave the house the following day, after the gurgling has subsided, I hide my American cash between the Barthes and the Baudelaire in my Aunt's bookshelf—just in case. I am slipping in and out of sleep with the gurgling that's turned into some kind of crunching because the baby, my baby, has started eating through the concrete. These old countryside houses in Medellin, built almost completely into the mountains. Tucked to be forgotten. My baby, she'll eat through the whole damn house into the mountain. Into the fucking earth.
So I press a pillow over my face but the placenta which I thought was like, maybe, a little bit myth is slithering out me like a wet ghost and I'm just not sure I'm going to be able to keep this thing hidden for very much longer. S had asked about the ummm, stress swelling, and I told him that nothing was wrong and to stop being so temperamental. And then it was out! It was out! She was out! Sliding all over the bed. The sheets. My placenta-- she was out but she was SO charming she started making wet noises in the dark of the room and I started mouthing, "STOP IT! STOP IT!" but while laughing so it was hard to discern my intention. Then my placenta, she's so funny, she crawled out the window and said LATER FUCKFACE— & the baby, my baby still eating at the walls making her way, closer, closer with every gorge.

WHERE ARE THE SOUNDS FOR WHEN YOU ENTER AND I ENTER AND ME AND MY FOUR AND A HALF LEGS COME TRAMPLE ON YOUR HEART WHEN I'M 28

[I am your almost fully grown abortion]
The first morning in this new country, my lover attempts to learn the language from the
local newspapers but can't look anyone in the eyes

I remember my dream of the books in the bedroom flapping their skewered lips at me
soaking me in the theory of the PAPA (or so I believe), so I can behave; I had a dress on
& when I lashed the good book against my bottom, my breasts, it was like the Madonna
video where she pretend-fucks the TV --- oh! and I shout MEDIA, MEDIA caress me too!

but how I'm feeling in the hammock waiting for Maria to beckon us to breakfast
this first morning, here, preening goodness is the real and true sickness:
why these limbs, this hair? I was once the perfect faceless ball of flesh
{pain is anachronistic} LONG LIVE THE NEW FLESH {{{{{Debbie Harry's mouth}}}}}}}}}}

my abortion is called to the kitchen & sits to eat the pankekees
I stumble upon the language gaze and fall into the coffee
pancakes are called pankekees in here- she flashes her box for proof-
the touch of the English on everything & my lover is baby goosebumping
at the feel of something round and familiar

The abortion chuckles with a sincerity

my grandmother Lion wants to talk death—she's been waiting my whole life
one can gut themselves under the table—I've seen it in movies—
grandmother, atemporal & spitting

                                        —telling me we all have rights
                                        to die!

the tiny abortions inside of me are trembling, sparkling
hot bulbous lights, salty & fresh
catching a glimpse of their own reflection in my grandmother

she doesn't have any pankekees & my lover can't stuff his mouth fast enough
his every orifice fully stuffed

the evening prior, before the dream, I had to touch every book in the room before I
could sleep
& kuss the inside of the pages
but those letters cut me, teetered & tethered me
the only real body is the cut body; {{{{{{{{{{{{{{I don't want to be here}}}}}}}}}}}}}}

you are a full grown abortion, I fell asleep thinking

running a finger over the creased copy of El extranjero

before stuffing it in my pajama pants

DADA CULTURES

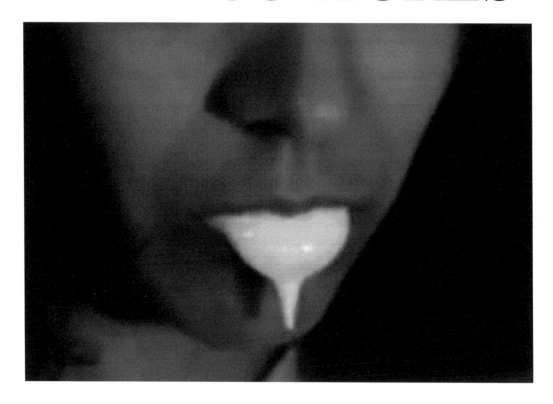

No to when i try to "see both sides"
I don't need to see all the sides, when one of the sides causes suffering
No to sides
No to angles
No to perspective
No to me
No to me
No to me when I compromise
No to that time I got drunk and was abusive
No to blaming my abuse on being drunk
No to being an abuser
No to no shame
No to no shame
No to no shame

WHEN I WAS LITTLE I KEPT YOUR PICTURE UNDER MY PILLOW BECAUSE I REALLY WANTED TO AND I THOUGHT THAT WAS WHAT I WAS SUPPOSED TO DO AND THEN WHEN I LOST IT I ONLY FELT SLIGHT OFF

So much blood in my memory stool

I'M NOT OKAY I tell the stewardess

& unhitch the little bathroom door lock; she brings in a box of tissues

and you clean up your bloody like a map

earholes and your mouth and even your fingertips

are covered

IT'S THE PRESSURE she says to you HAPPENS TO EVERYONE

You feel so lucky to have her you kiss her on the mouth

And she says MA'AM! But the other's luggage

She gives you a list of unconjugated verbs to repeat

& you say THANK YOU

you want her to make you feel like you're the only girl in the world

but it's clear that there's no WE here, there's barely an I

Jennifer, look at the chair

Look at the chair
Look at the chair
Look at the chair
In the chair is your father
What do you want to say to your fatherchair

The goodlooking face tumble out of you
And you cover it with the best gunk and stuff
http://www.sephora.com/velvet-matte-lip-pencil-P78834
http://www.sephora.com/illuminator-P284301?skuId=1307552
http://www.sephora.com/speckled-nail-varnish-P377106?skuId=1481332

You cover the fatherchair in cusses
And say I love you fatherchair how I miss you fatherchair
And you kiss & kiss & kiss until the fatherchair is over
Your mouth is over

There's no WE here, there's barely an I

Did you lose your yet face, Jennifer

you did not practice
& the thing that tumbles out of you
when you first see him
in the trembling moment of first embrace
is not a part of you
but a version of you that the word defaults to
a verse of you that you saw on this one website

WHAT MOVIES DO YOU LIKE WATCHING & WHAT DO YOU MAKE OF YOUR OTHER SONS

slight pleasures to playing the aggressor

                    pretty please stick your white in me?

& maybe we'll see yourself better

There's a WE here, there's almost an I

Is there anything that's not about pain? If so, speak it into my mouth.

Spit it into my mouth.

LIFE DOESN'T MAKE SENSE BECAUSE THE INTERNET
DOESN'T MAKE SENSE—
AGREE OR DISAGREE

Jennifer Tamayo

March 7 · AddThis Sharing ·

Wondering, again, why it takes this level of exposure for survivors to be listened to and believed?What is it about details of abuse that makes people say: I believe you; I will do something. Wondering how many people and institutions looked the other way for many, many years?? Will Cave Canem respond? Will the Iowa Writers' Workshop? Sending love and support for those coming forward.

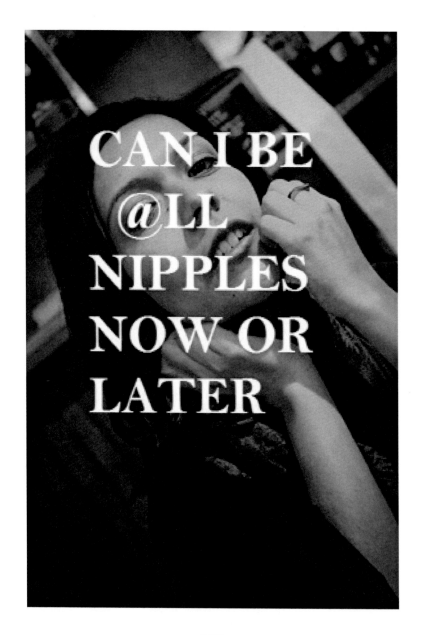

I have tried to know you better in my imagination—I won't apologize
The spit comes out all bloody mixed with suds and spit and come
& his mother says that's a lot of come & my brother says I'm going
to have to tell mom that you are sick
I tried to spittle it right into the black hole so as to hide
But it was no use since it all splattered against the porcelain white
All we have left to do is to strike out at life

my parts would do nothing to animate—I AM NOT ME
I sit on his face while the other blows him and I had to put my bow
back on because there was another man in the room probably watching
When I spit into the sink I'm writing you the best poem
I can come though I'm riding the man's face gracefully
I'm thinking about my stockings; I'll just DIE
if they rip and about how this pleasure described in this poem will read nothing like the earth
why must everything be communicated

When I inspect my labia in the morning—I remember that this is likely not my own either
Temperamental Temperamental—I AM NOT ME
When my vagina had been close to swallowing the head of the sweet, sweet boy I decided
I didn't want to split myself so I splot and ask that one sucks the other while I watch
& can I gently strum myself; the man watching doesn't approve;
Freedom and destruction gyrate in a perfect fix

the gaze is plural because of the nature of looking

my eye ball fell out of my face and splintered

and not splintered—was as it always was

was as it always will be

there's no WE here, there's barely an I

No to the thing I'm doing now to absolve myself
No to your tenderness towards me
No to no tenderness
No to liberation without destruction
No to no self- destruction; I need to be abolished

AIMÉ CÉSAIRE IS A PERSON I'D LIKE YOU TO READ BEFORE I ARRIVE
& THEN I ARRIVE

Como negocian diferencias culturales a cerca de como se deben criar los niños:

Animar
Prolongar
Poner en practica
Ingreso
Apoyar
Ganar
Sacar provecho
Creencias
Establecer

Consider your relationships with the people you organize events with. Are they committed to creating spaces that are safe(r), equitable, and liberatory? If not, why are you continuing to organize with them?

from "Call to Action" handout from the Enough is Enough collective, distributed to participants in a town-hall meeting held at St. Mark's Poetry Project, New York City, on November 6, 2014.

when we create distance from one thing, say "an audience" or say "a chair," we get closer to something else say, "the other chair" or say "euphoria"

Make it nauseous, I'm traveling in time

DO YOU WANT TO DANCE WITH SOMEBODY?
SOMEBODY WHO LOVES YOU?

A BOOK EXISTS HERE THAT I CAN SHOVE IN THIS WORD HOLE

On my first night I dose off rubbing the spine of El Extranjero with the tip of my index fatter. this book feels like a wishhook. I image it wearing a little somber. and I get the tingle in the back of my throat. Mama murio hoy. Mama se murio hoy. Hoy murio mama. Hoy mama se murio. Murio hoy, mama. Hoy, mama murio. Did I always know how to pray. I should get up and write this, I think. I should get up and write, like I do.

No to not the masters' tools; maybe they look different in my hands
No to not the masters' tools; maybe they transform my hands
No to the master
No to masters classes
No to mastery
No to masters programs
No to self-mastery
No to masters. PERIOD.

THE QUESTIONS, DADDY, COME PLUNGING OUT ME FROM THE TOILET VOWEL OF OUR HISTORY!

At one point I find myself in a hot tub with my father. Beyond the pool on the other side of the courtyard, the rest of our family sits in the shade of a tree with vibrant, red flowers and fruit so hot it's rotting right on the branch. If there's any intimate moment in the world, if there was one moment in my life in which I should connect to another person—this might be it. But the sun is throwing up all over me and I am hoping my flesh will get eaten by the chlorine in the tub and I can be a little shimmerwound in the water. My father has freckles on his chest and his face is full like a hot bladder. Who is going to eat me? Who is going to eat me now? The red flower with all its terrible petals grows as large as the world and we are all suddenly very dead and very hungry. There is no earth, no time, only the dead zombie flower body and us, its zombie babies. To have so many petals is a very encouraging thing and when I find my real dead body in the landscape, by the side of the hot tub I eat it with great pleasure... Back in the tub, I consider just drowning myself; I'm looking at my father's freckles like they were some kind of sun, some kind of meaning but I can't help think of his penis just a few spaces away. The way I think of every penis when I think of a man. They way I'm thinking of your penis right now. & your other penis. & the flower's penis. & the hot tub's penis. & my grandmother's penis. The way every penis in the world just seems to fill me at every moment. Piercing me from the inside out. I want to ask you how your organs fall out of you but that red flower bladder slaps me, digs its petals into my glowing belly, piercing me until I'm just a surface, a scrap of flesh caught between pricks.

I TAKE A TELESCOPE TO THE SHAPE AND SIZE OF YOUR ORGANS
THOSE I CAN'T SEE

TQM. YES, EVERYTHINGS REALLY GOOD. BUSY WITH WORK
BUT THAT's HOW I LIKE IT. THE WEATHER IS OKAY. &
TQM. YES, EVERYTHINGS REALLY GOOD. BUSY WITH WORK
BUT THAT's HOW I LIKE IT. THE WEATHER IS OKAY. &
TQM. YES, EVERYTHINGS REALLY GOOD. BUSY WITH WORK
BUT THAT's HOW I LIKE IT. THE WEATHER IS OKAY. &
TQM. YES, EVERYTHINGS REALLY GOOD. BUSY WITH WORK
BUT THAT's HOW I LIKE IT. THE WEATHER IS OKAY. &
TQM. YES, EVERYTHINGS REALLY GOOD. BUSY WITH WORK
BUT THAT's HOW I LIKE IT. THE WEATHER IS OKAY. &
TQM. YES, EVERYTHINGS REALLY GOOD. BUSY WITH WORK
BUT THAT's HOW I LIKE IT. THE WEATHER IS OKAY. &
TQM. YES, EVERYTHINGS REALLY GOOD. BUSY WITH WORK
BUT THAT's HOW I LIKE IT. THE WEATHER IS OKAY. &
TQM. YES, EVERYTHINGS REALLY GOOD. BUSY WITH WORK
BUT THAT's HOW I LIKE IT. THE WEATHER IS OKAY. &
TQM. YES, EVERYTHINGS REALLY GOOD. BUSY WITH WORK
BUT THAT's HOW I LIKE IT. THE WEATHER IS OKAY. &
TQM. YES, EVERYTHINGS REALLY GOOD. BUSY WITH WORK
BUT THAT's HOW I LIKE IT. THE WEATHER IS OKAY. &
TQM. YES, EVERYTHINGS REALLY GOOD. BUSY WITH WORK
BUT THAT's HOW I LIKE IT. THE WEATHER IS OKAY. &
TQM. YES, EVERYTHINGS REALLY GOOD. BUSY WITH WORK
BUT THAT's HOW I LIKE IT. THE WEATHER IS OKAY. &
TQM. YES, EVERYTHINGS REALLY GOOD. BUSY WITH WORK
BUT THAT's HOW I LIKE IT. THE WEATHER IS OKAY. &

TQM. YES, EVERYTHINGS REALLY GOOD. BUSY WITH WORK
BUT THAT's HOW I LIKE IT. THE WEATHER IS OKAY. &
TQM. YES, EVERYTHINGS REALLY GOOD. BUSY WITH WORK
BUT THAT's HOW I LIKE IT. THE WEATHER IS OKAY. &
TQM. YES, EVERYTHINGS REALLY GOOD. BUSY WITH WORK
BUT THAT's HOW I LIKE IT. THE WEATHER IS OKAY. &
TQM. YES, EVERYTHINGS REALLY GOOD. BUSY WITH WORK
BUT THAT's HOW I LIKE IT. THE WEATHER IS OKAY. &
TQM. YES, EVERYTHINGS REALLY GOOD. BUSY WITH WORK
BUT THAT's HOW I LIKE IT. THE WEATHER IS OKAY. &

i sit down at the counter. i order pancakes. i put on sunglasses. i look pretty. i am in between two older men. i hear one man say to me you are between us but don't worry you are safe. then he adds well maybe not. i can't look him in the face. i am too hungry. i don't want to talk. everyone is looking at me with the men. the other man is quiet. he's a veteran, he saved our lives says the first man. remember when you played soccer with the germans. i don't want to talk. i can feel his weight on the stool. i study the menu gratuitously. i think about bacon. i think about oatmeal. i think about writing. i pour a fistful of sugar into my coffee. i drink my coffee.

the second man leaves when my pancakes arrive and the first man opens his newspaper and says let's see what we see. he notices my ring. he says it looks nice. he says i should wear it on my right hand so I can defend myself. i tell him i'm left handed. he asks me to make a fist. to show it to him. he studies my fist. he says good. he says i should practice and punch my pillow. he says women are getting raped and killed out here. he says the city is unsafe. he says there are no jobs. he says it will get worse. he says i need to practice my punching. he says i need to get one of these. he points to his pocket. he points to a metal thing. he says do you know what this is. he says i'll show you what this this is. he takes it out. he opens it up. he shows me the blade. the blade catches the light. he makes me afraid. the blade makes me afraid. he says you'll need one when you get stabbed one day. he says it's not hard to stab after you've been stabbed. he says i don't need to go out anymore. he says don't go out at night. he says now i have the internet. he points to my laptop on the countertop.

i get the good butter. i put the butter on my pancakes. i cover the pancakes in syrup and butter. i feel like i'm going to have to throw this up. i eat the pancakes. i think about throwing up the pancakes. i eat the pancakes. i have cramps. i am going to get my period, i think. i am a whale. i am a big bloody animal.

he opens to a page with a photo of the late Whitney Houston wearing a snake print dress. he says i'm going to get you that snake print dress. he says would you like that dress. he hears me say thank you. he picks up his pen to cut out the image. he stops himself. he turns the page. he says you can eat the good butter because you are spanish. he says we can eat anything we want we will live until we are 89, you and i. he says what sign are you. he say's me too. he says oh you like looking at the moon and all that shit. you love looking at the moon and you like lightning at night. he says you also love pens and notebooks. you are obsessed with pens.

you keep a diary don't you? you are obsessed with pens and notebooks. go to this website he says. they have all these pens and notebooks. he shows me his pen. he says he goes out at night to look at the moon. do you keep a diary he says. he says me too. he says he has eight journals. he says we are the same. he says he likes the snow. he says he likes the snow at night. he says i like it too. he says i shouldn't believe in that stuff too much. he says i only believe in it a little. he knows i agree. he says we also like milk. he says he knows me. he uses the word envidia. he says tu sabes. he tells me about a place down town with good milk. he has a cap and a mustache. he is a stranger.

i know this stranger. i become a very large thing. i can feel my bones filling with milk. i can see his car from where we sit. i like his car. it's white. it looks clean. i want to touch this man's hair. i want to touch the fat that is spilling from the stool. i want to touch his shoes. i ask him how old he thinks i am. i am surprised when he says 32. i hear him call me honey. i don't stop him. i want to ask about his family but he's giving me advice about money. i am supposed to put 40% of my paycheck away. i can feel the blade in his pants. i think i should move tables. that voice is telling me to move tables. i cry one tear into my pancakes. i can feel the blade through his pants. i find out he's not married. never married. no kids. never wanted to. says he'd rather go to the movies alone. he

Jennifer Tamayo

October 26, 2014 ·

the feminists are coming to fuck some shit up, nyc poetry scene. luvubye.

says don't get married, honey. he says you'll be happier alone. you can go to the movies alone.

when the gypsies enter he says honey those are gypsies. he looks for my purse. he moves it closer to me. i let him. i see the gypsies. her hair is the color of fake orange. i had hair like that once. he says move your phone from the edge of the counter honey. he says it's going to fall. i move the phone. i put it on my laptop. he says thats better. i let him say that's better to me. i am the pancake. i say you didn't read my horoscope. he tries to read it. he reads you size up the situation and reconsider. don't let anyone change your plans. someone will try to change your plans. he skips the words he can't read. he skips one sentence. he asks if i graduated high school. he says i should go into law enforcement. after 9/11 everyone's afraid. he says there's money there.

estas calmada i hear him say. me, honey. when a woman is is violent. i consider getting in consider the blade. i consider consider the blade. i consider blade. i consider the blade. consider the blade. i consider

he says i hope you learned something from violent is it different than when a man the white car. i consider the blade. i the blade. i consider the blade. i the blade. i consider the blade. i consider the i consider the blade. i consider the blade. i staying all day.

124

No to having to tell our rape stories
No to having to tell our harassment stories
No to being asked for the details

From no manifesto for poetry readings and listservs and magazines and "open versatile spaces where cultural production flourishes" after Yvonne Rainer

Signed: a crowd of feminists based in Baltimore, MD, US Berkeley, CA, US Brighton, United Kingdom Hamilton, ON, Canada London, United Kingdom Melbourne, Australia New York, NY, US Oxford, OH, US Oakland, CA, U.S. San Francisco, CA, US Vancouver, BC, Canada lacking consensus and okay with that

IN THE INSTANCE THAT YOU ARE THE REAL FATHER—HOW SHOULD THE REAL WOMAN UH…

This tall, female, very well endowed mannequin on her sturdy metal base is quite a looker—both body and face; she seems to meet society's "ideal" of the incredibly slim, large-breasted, tall woman. She is not flimsy plastic but constructed of a much more substantial plaster-based material that enables her to hold together while being manipulated and renders her heavier than plastic.

Her face is modestly made up; her smooth bald head accommodates head pieces or wigs of any type. She comes with punky, two-tone wig shown in first photo. Her arms, hands, torso, and one leg detach from metal pegs; her left leg and bottom below torso slide down onto metal stand. She cannot stand on her own.

Measurements (total height: 5' 1.3")
Head--circumference around top of skull: 19.5"
Torso--length from top of head to waist: 29"; circumference around breasts at nipple level: 38"; shoulder span: 15"; shoulder to hand detachment: 19.5"; shoulder to tip of fingers: 28"; waist: 23"; hips: 31"
Legs--longest piece (from separation at hip/torso to bottom of left foot): 42"
Base--base height: 12"; diameter: 14"
Weight: 25 lbs

This item ships USPS Standard Post due to size, weight, and packaging requirements-- torso and head may ship separately from limbs and base if sizing restrictions require. Shipping quote derives from USPS rate charts and is based on the furthest location from Alabama. Shipping overages, which are likely for those east of Texas, will be refunded to buyer. Convo first with zip code if you would prefer an exact quote to your location. Please convo with additional questions.

$275.00 USD

Only 1 available

Add to Cart

Favorite

....UH UH UH UH UH UH ACT

uuhh uhhh you, the daughter, walk through a pebbled obstacle course
El Parque de Piez Descalzos.

the game in which the father and the brother and the lover guide you
with their voices across the stone path
& you are barefoot
& you are blindfolded
& this is not to be a tortured type of porn
more poetic irony cuz
you are in another country,
                    like an other's country.
                            like the country of the most others in your life
                            like the most tortured type of porn
                            pleasure is not pleasure everywhere

 a place to connect with the soil, the land
you crook the world inside of you, daughter

WHAT WAS YOUR FIRST WORD—SHOW ME HOW IT TUMBLED OUT YOU

- addicted to male attention **wildflower44** 3/9/06
- Re: addicted to male attention **jtamayo** 3/10/06
- Re: addicted to male attention » jonquiljo **wildflower44** 3/10/06
- Re: addicted to male attention **jtamayo** 3/10/06
- Re: addicted to male attention » wildflower44 **Tamar** 3/11/06
- Re: addicted to male attention **Cici** 7/8/06
- Re: addicted to male attention **rfs** 9/3/06
- Re: addicted to male attention **tinkerbelle06** 9/25/08
- Re: addicted to male attention **kposs75** 12/24/08

If you are in a position of hiring or promoting and you are made aware of wrongdoing (assault, harassment, discrimination, etc.), be prepared to take steps that could be publicly messy in order to make change. There are people who abuse positions of power, who still get invited to do readings, to teach, to publish, to mentor, who still have careers, because of a status quo silence or worse, fear or passivity. Are you willing to fire someone or otherwise refuse to bolster the career or legacy of an abuser? If not, consider whom and what you are protecting.

from "Call to Action" handout from the Enough is Enough collective, distributed to participants in a town-hall meeting held at St. Mark's Poetry Project, New York City, on November 6, 2014.

[No gentle part of the artist said Artaud]

DESCRIBE THIS MYTH WITH OUR COUNTRY'S INFLECTIONS

I tried to see myself so clearly I didn't see myself. [

The mariachi was looking at my big face

Daddy and I were reliving all the things we had missed

Like a quinceañera at 29

But when someone looks at your face you are a little more dead

than you were before

You find it, your face and you just say—that's not me

Jennifer Tamayo

July 15, 2015 ·

NEW MOON FEVER: If you needed REAL PROOF in order to stand with survivors-- you are not standing with survivors, you are standing with the cops. If you were skeptical of The Invisibles' letter until a specific person came forward to you under your terms, you supported rape culture. If you gleefully welcomed back the editor that sent me and 11 other women legally threatening letters, you didn't stand with survivors and you looked the other way. If you were conveniently "conflicted" until a couple of feminist poets stepped away from _____ press, you did not stand with survivors, you were a bystander. If your first instinct is to publicly post "POOR ME," you are not standing with survivors, you are standing with yourself. SIDE-EYE FOREVA.

WHAT COLOR IS THE INNER LINING OF YOUR DRESS

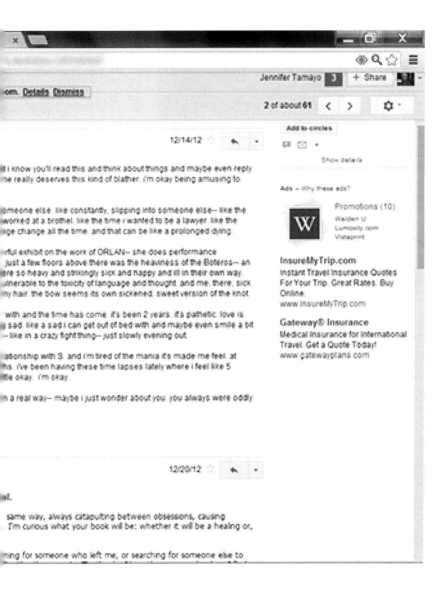

12/14/12

i know you'll read this and think about things and maybe even reply.
he really deserves this kind of blather. i'm okay being amusing to

omeone else. like constantly. slipping into someone else-- like the
worked at a brothel. like the time i wanted to be a lawyer. like the
nge change all the time. and that can be like a prolonged dying

rful exhibit on the work of ORLAN-- she does performance
just a few floors above there was the heaviness of the Boteros-- an
re so heavy and strikingly sick and happy and ill in their own way.
ulnerable to the toxicity of language and thought. and me, there, sick
ny hair. the bow seems its own sickened, sweet version of the knot.

with and the time has come. it's been 2 years. it's pathetic. love is
g sad. like a sad i can get out of bed with and maybe even smile a bit
-- like in a crazy fight thing-- just slowly evening out.

ationship with S. and i'm tired of the mania it's made me feel. at
hs. i've been having these time lapses lately where i feel like 5
ttle okay. i'm okay.

h a real way-- maybe i just wonder about you. you always were oddly

12/20/12

al.

same way, always catapulting between obsessions, causing
I'm curious what your book will be: whether it will be a healing or,

ning for someone who left me, or searching for someone else to

Consider doing the right thing. Consider saying something. Consider being true to yourself. Consider being true to others. Consider burning bridges. Consider the possibility that it doesn't have to be this way forever.

from "Call to Action" handout from the Enough is Enough collective, distributed to participants in a town-hall meeting held at St. Mark's Poetry Project, New York City, on November 6, 2014.

WHAT IS DESIRE

UH UH UH UH UH UH UH UH UH

**MY STUDENT THOUGHT IMMIGRANT WAS A DIRTY WORD—
WHAT DOES MY STUDENT THINK OF FATHER**

THIS IS THE BELLY I CAN DIG MYSELF OUT

Want you to make me feel like I'm the only girl in the world
Like I'm the only one that you'll ever know
Like I'm the only one that knows your heart
Like I'm the only one that's in command
Cause I'm the only one that understands how
To make you feel like a man

No to thinking any of this will be resolved without pain
No to no pain
No to no pain
No to no pain
No to self-care, there are parts of me that don't deserve care
No to self-care, i can dismantle legacies by dismantling myself
No to self-care, if it means avoiding conflict
No to self-care if it means avoiding discomfort

No to no self-care, part of me should live
No to no self-care, parts of you should live

I'VE GOTTEN SO FAT ON THE INTERNET
I CANNOT PUT MY DRESS ON

Special Notes & Thanks

YOU DA ONE was largely composed between July 2012 and July 2013—following my return to my native country Colombia after 25 years. The project is deeply indebted to and inspired by Rihanna, Roland Barthes's *Mourning Diary*, and Aimé Césaire's *Cahier d'un Retour au Pays Natal*, whose words appear on pages 24, 35, 74, and 109. The work of Débora Arango, Orlan, and Fernando Botero are also of note. This 2017 edition was edited between 2015 and 2016 following a change in publishers.

In addition to the editors and curators who featured early sections and performances of this project and those thanked in the first edition, much gratitude to the friends and artists whose care supported me through the completion of this iteration of YOU DA ONE: Eunsong Kim, Nikki Wallschlaeger, Becca Klaver, Sade Murphy, Lucas de Lima, suit sister Lauren Traetto, Vanessa Angelica Villarreal, Wo Chan, Jess X. Chen, Lara Weibgen, those who were part of NYCs Enough is Enough meetings in 2015, the collaborative writings from the 'crowds of feminists lacking consensus;' and thank you late night circles of survivors across lands and times and wires, for holding me and each other.

A very special thank you to Carmen Giménez-Smith for making another home for YOU DA ONE when I couldn't really imagine one. Suzi F. Garcia and Sarah Gzemski, thank you for your labor, your feedback, and your patience with me and the restaging of this book. Your tenderness has been so important to me.

Lastly, this book is still for Sol Angela Tamayo Silva and the beautiful library of ancestral mothers always waiting for me in the mountains in Medellín.